CRYPTOLOGY

SECRETS OF NAVAJO CODE TALKERS

RACHAEL L. THOMAS

Lerner Publications ◆ Minneapolis

Lerner Publications Company
An imprint of Lerner Publishing Group, Inc.
241 First Avenue North
Minneapolis, MN 55401 USA

For reading levels and more information, look up this title at www.lernerbooks.com.

Main body text set in Aptifer Sans LT Pro
Typeface provided by Linotype

The images in this book are used with the permission of: © Joesboy/Getty Images, pp. 3, 11; © PhotoQuest/Getty Images, p. 4; © Historical/Getty Images, pp. 5, 22; © Everett Collection/Shutterstock Images, pp. 6–8, 23; © Nastasic/Getty Images, p. 9; © grandriver/Getty Images, pp. 10, 18; © Fort Worth Star-Telegram/Getty Images, pp. 12–13; © Horace Bristol/Getty Images, p. 14; © National Archives and Records Administration, pp. 15–17, 20, 24, 27; © Picsfive/Shutterstock Images, pp. 19, 29; © Bettmann/Getty Images, p. 21; © Interim Archives/Getty Images, p. 25; © Photo 12/Getty Images, p. 26; © MIKE THEILER/Getty Images, p. 28.

Cover Photo: © National Archives and Records Administration

Design Elements: © AF-studio/Getty Images; © 4khz/Getty Images; © non-exclusive/Getty Images

Library of Congress Cataloging-in-Publication Data

Names: Thomas, Rachael L., author.
Title: Secrets of Navajo code talkers / Rachael L. Thomas.
Description: Minneapolis : Lerner Publications, [2022] | Series: Cryptology (alternator books ®) | Includes bibliographical references and index. | Audience: Ages 8–12 | Audience: Grades 4–6 | Summary: "Cryptology was key to the success of the Battle of Iwo Jima during World War II. Learn more in this introduction to the Navajo and why and how their language was well-suited to being used for coded messages."— Provided by publisher.
Identifiers: LCCN 2020019932 (print) | LCCN 2020019933 (ebook) | ISBN 9781728404592 (library binding) | ISBN 9781728417981 (ebook)
Subjects: LCSH: World War, 1939–1945—Cryptography—Juvenile literature. | Navajo code talkers—Juvenile literature. | Navajo language—Juvenile literature. | World War, 1939–1945—Participation, Indian—Juvenile literature. | United States. Marine Corps—Indian troops—History—20th century—Juvenile literature.
Classification: LCC D810.C88 T46 2021 (print) | LCC D810.C88 (ebook) | DDC 940.54/8673—dc23

LC record available at https://lccn.loc.gov/2020019932
LC ebook record available at https://lccn.loc.gov/2020019933

Manufactured in the United States of America
2-1008943-49031-9/27/2022

TABLE OF CONTENTS

INTRODUCTION

It is February 1945. A battle rages on the Pacific island of Iwo Jima. Thousands of marines storm the island's shores. Thousands of Japanese troops lie in wait, hidden in the thick jungle.

A US commander studies the battlefield and decides where troops and ammunition are needed. He relays these orders to a pair of Navajo soldiers sheltered in a small dugout. The two soldiers are surrounded by wires and radio equipment. One soldier speaks into the radio in a language the commander does not understand.

Japanese code breakers don't understand it either. In the three years the United States has been fighting in World War II (1939–1945), enemy troops have failed to crack the complex Navajo language. Every day, the Navajo code talkers help ensure US victory.

A group of code talkers in 1942

The battle of Iwo Jima was one of World War II's bloodiest battles.

AMERICA AT WAR

In 1939, World War II broke out across Europe. It began with Germany invading Poland on September 1. Two days later, Great Britain and France responded by declaring war on Germany.

The United States did not join the war at first. Some Americans wanted to help fight against Germany. Others wanted to stay neutral.

As the war intensified, staying neutral became more difficult. Germany continued to invade European territories. The Japanese military had also joined German forces. President Franklin D. Roosevelt grew worried that Japanese troops would attack the United States.

On December 7, 1941, Japan bombed Pearl Harbor, a US military base in Hawaii. The United States could no longer stay out of the war. The next day, the US Congress declared war on Japan and Germany.

German soldiers invade Poland in 1939.

More than 2,000 people died in the attack on Pearl Harbor.

Enigma machines were used by the Germans to send ciphered messages during World War II.

For thousands of years, military leaders have relied on the ability to send and receive secret messages during war. The science of secret communication is called cryptology. Cryptology has helped win many battles! Like many warring countries during World War II, the United States used math and technology to scramble messages. Machines were built to encipher important communications. However, using complex cipher systems was slow compared to regular speech. So, the US military also relied on the Navajo language to protect secret messages.

STEAM Spotlight—Technology

During World War II, Germany's cipher system was transmitted using devices called Enigma machines. Enigma machines used scrambler disks to encipher messages. The scrambler disks constantly rotated. This altered the cipher system even as a message was being written!

Julius Caesar was one of the first military leaders to use secret messages in battle.

9

THE NAVAJO PEOPLE

When Pearl Harbor was bombed in 1941, the US military had 2.2 million soldiers. The government hurried to draft and train more men. Included in this number were tens of thousands of American Indians. Some of those drafted were Navajo.

In the 1940s, most Navajos lived in the Navajo Nation. This reservation stretched across Utah, Arizona, and New Mexico. Very few people lived on the reservation who were not Navajo. So, the Navajo language was rarely heard or understood by people outside of the Navajo Nation. This later helped make Navajo the perfect code.

The Navajo Nation is the largest reservation in the United States.

A code talker monument in Window Rock, Arizona. Window Rock is the capital of the Navajo Nation.

Choctaw code talker Tobias Frazier received an honorable discharge from the military following a period of faithful service.

The US military had used American Indian languages as secret codes for many years. In World War I (1914–1918), the Choctaw people served as code talkers in several battles.

The Choctaw code talkers sent messages to one another in their native language. This helped keep important information safe from enemy troops. German soldiers who listened in on the messages couldn't understand the language! The success of the Choctaw code talkers led some to believe that other American Indian languages could be used in World War II.

CRYPTO SPOTLIGHT

Nineteen Choctaw soldiers served in World War I. They formed a communications team called the Choctaw Telephone Squad. Code talkers from the Telephone Squad were stationed on front lines and at command posts.

Members of the Choctaw code talkers

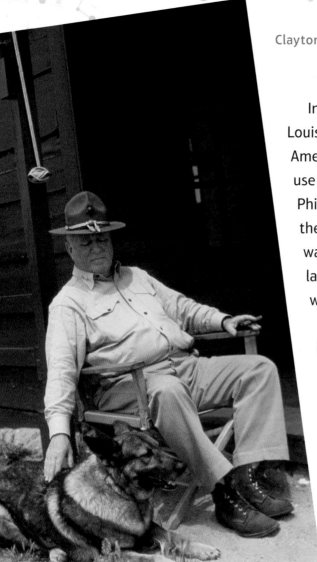

Clayton B. Vogel

In 1942, an army division in Louisiana began testing other American Indian languages to use as codes. Army veteran Philip Johnston read about the division's tests. Johnston was familiar with the Navajo language and thought it would make a good code.

Johnston demonstrated his idea to Major James E. Jones and General Clayton B. Vogel. During the demonstration, four Navajo translated messages from English to Navajo to English again. It took them minutes. By applying complex ciphers, soldiers would have taken hours to complete the translations! Johnston's idea of creating a code from the Navajo language was soon approved.

CRYPTO SPOTLIGHT

Philip Johnston was born in 1892 in Topeka, Kansas. At the age of four, Johnston's family moved to Arizona, where his parents worked on the Navajo reservation. There, Johnston learned the Navajo language.

The Commandant, U.S. Marine Corps, page 2

Recently, I made a trip to San Diego for the purpose of learning what progress had been made in utilizing the Navajo language for communication. Colonel Jones told me that the plan had been tried out with a limited number of Indians, had proved highly successful, and that he had requested authority to enlist additional personnel. I inquired if, in his opinion, my services could be utilized in the training of Navajos. His reply was a decided affirmative. He suggested that I contact the recruiting officer here, bearing in mind that I would need authorization to serve both inside and outside continental United States with the Indians.

Because of my great desire to be of service in the foregoing capacity, and to get started in this work at the earliest possible moment, I am applying for enlistment in the Marine Corps rather than for a commission, which would entail more time and uncertainty. As a further means of saving time, I have taken my physical examination at the local recruiting office, the results of which are shown on the inclosed application.

I have taken the liberty to explain in some detail the basis upon which I request favorable action from your office. I have marked the application "urgent" at the suggestion of the local recruiting officer, since my understanding of Navajo psychology would make me of value in the immediate future during recruiting of the new Indian personnel.

Very truly yours,

Philip Johnston
Philip Johnston

In 1942, Johnston enlisted in the US Marines to help recruit and train code talkers.

BUILDING
THE CODE

In the summer of 1942, twenty-nine Navajos were recruited by the US Marines. The recruits quickly got to work building a code system into the Navajo language.

Navajo was ideal for building a secret code for many reasons. Few people knew the language. At the time, the US government estimated only twenty-eight non-Navajo Americans understood it. The syntax of the Navajo language was also extremely complex. So, it would be difficult for someone to learn the language quickly.

Navajo is historically a spoken language. At the time, there was no official Navajo alphabet. This also made cracking the code more difficult, as there were no written resources to help someone learn the language.

STEAM Spotlight—Art

Oral storytelling is an important part of Navajo culture. A common theme in stories is the link between nature and people.

The twenty-nine Navajo recruits are sworn in as marines.

17

The Navajo call their language *Diné Bizaad*, or the "People's Language."

The Navajo code would be used to send messages containing military terms. However, these words and phrases did not exist in the Navajo language. So, one of the Navajo recruits' first tasks was to add military meaning to normal Navajo vocabulary.

Much of this vocabulary was about nature. Submarines were called "iron fish" in Navajo code. Battleships were "whales," and grenades were "potatoes." When complete, the Navajo military code had 211 words.

The Navajo recruits also created a way to spell out words letter by letter. Each letter of the English alphabet was first assigned an animal whose name began with that letter. For example, *a* was assigned "ant." The Navajo translation of the word "ant," *wol-la-chee*, signified *a* when used in the code.

THE NAVAJO CODE

Military Terms

CODE WORD	NAVAJO WORD	MEANING
tortoise	*chay-da-gahi*	tank
rabbit trail	*gah-bih-tkeen*	route
two stars	*so-na-kih*	Major general

Alphabet Terms

LETTER	NAVAJO WORD	ENGLISH WORD
a	*wol-la-chee*	ant
b	*shush*	bear
c	*moasi*	cat

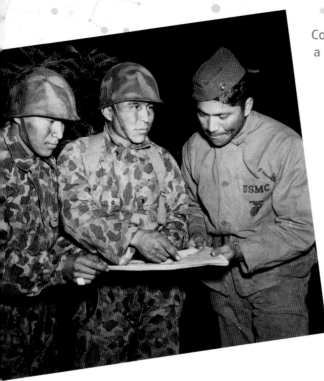

Code talkers study a problem at a US Marines training school.

After the code was made, more Navajos were recruited and trained as code talkers. Learning the code took thirteen weeks. In addition, all Navajo soldiers spent seven weeks learning military procedure. Navajo code talkers also learned how to send and receive messages using complex radio equipment. The code talkers were responsible for setting up communication lines. And, they had to carry heavy radio packs on their backs as they moved from place to place.

STEAM Spotlight—Technology

World War II triggered a rapid development in radio technology. This included radar. Radar works by sending out radio waves. The waves reflect off distant objects, alerting troops to unseen figures. Naval officers used radar to detect other submarines. Radar was also used to detect bomber planes.

A marine trains in camouflage at a training base.

CHAPTER 4

NAVAJO CODE IN BATTLE

The code talkers first joined the US Marines in the Battle of Guadalcanal in August 1942. At first, the other marines were suspicious of the new recruits. They did not understand what the code talkers were doing. But as the code talkers got to work, the value of the Navajo code became clear.

In February 1943, the United States declared victory at Guadalcanal. Major General Alexander Vandegrift had led US troops during the battle. Vandegrift had been impressed by the Navajo code. So, he requested more code talkers!

The Battle of Guadalcanal was World War II's first major Pacific battle.

CRYPTO SPOTLIGHT

Chester Nez was one of the original twenty-nine Navajo recruits. He helped build the Navajo code when he was still a teenager. In 2011, he published *Code Talker*, a book about his life and wartime experiences. Nez passed away in 2014 at the age of 93.

Chester Nez in 2002

Code talkers Preston Toledo (*left*) and Frank Toledo work together to send and receive messages.

Code talker Carl Gorman surveys a hill during battle in 1944.

The Navajo code talkers were deployed in every major US Marine operation in the Pacific theater. The code talkers worked in teams of two. One code talker relayed and received messages. The other manned the portable radio and took notes.

The Navajo often relayed bombing coordinates. They also communicated troop movements and requests for supplies. The code talkers were almost always busy. They sometimes relayed messages for twenty-four hours straight!

The code talkers worked in dangerous situations. After each transmission, they moved to a new position to avoid Japanese fire. No matter what, the code talkers had to avoid capture. Any Navajo captured by enemy troops might be tortured to reveal the secrets of the code.

American troops raise
a flag during the
Battle of Iwo Jima.

The code talkers sometimes had to cut through dense jungle before they could operate their radio equipment.

Navajo code talkers served in several important battles in the Pacific theater. One was the Battle of Iwo Jima. Iwo Jima is an island located 750 miles (1,207 km) from Japan.

At the time, Iwo Jima had three airfields. The United States believed gaining control of these airfields would be useful for future battles. The US Marines invaded the island on February 19, 1945.

Six code talkers sent more than 800 messages during the Battle of Iwo Jima. Over the course of the five-week battle, the US Marines suffered heavy losses. But the code talkers helped the United States win. A military officer at Iwo Jima said that without the code talkers, the US Marines could not have won the battle.

Code talker John Brown Jr. (*left*) receives a gold Congressional Medal of Honor from President George W. Bush.

CONCLUSION

The Navajo code was never broken during World War II. It is the only modern military code to have never been cracked! After the war, the US government kept the secret of the Navajo code talkers classified for more than twenty years. But in 1968, their story was revealed.

In 2001, four surviving code talkers from the original twenty-nine recruits received the gold Congressional Medal of Honor. The bravery of the Navajo code talkers was finally recognized and celebrated.

Crack It! Translate Coded Messages →

Use the key below to translate messages spelled in Navajo code:

1. Dibeh ah-jah tsah be dibeh shi-da cla-gi-aih cla-gi-aih
   dibeh-yazzi tkin ah-jah dibeh
2. Ah-jah tsah ah-jah tsin-tliti tsah-as-zih wol-la-chee
   tse-gah ah-jah wol-la-chee be

NAVAJO WORD	ENGLISH WORD	LETTER
wol-la-chee	ant	a
be	deer	d
ah-jah	ear	e
tse-gah	hair	h
tkin	ice	i
dibeh-yazzi	lamb	l
tsin-tliti	match	m
tsah	needle	n
cla-gi-aih	pant	p
dibeh	sheep	s
shi-da	uncle	u
tsah-as-zih	yucca	y

GLOSSARY

airfield: a field where airplanes take off and land

cipher: a message in which individual letters are changed to conceal the message's meaning

classified: kept secret from most people

code: a message in which words or phrases are changed to conceal the message's meaning. A code breaker is someone who cracks codes.

draft: to select for mandatory military service. To be selected is to be drafted.

encipher: to hide the meaning of a message using a cipher

key: the tool or resource that helps a person decode or decipher a hidden message

neutral: not taking a side

oral: spoken and not written

reservation: an area of public land managed by an American Indian tribe

syntax: the way in which words are put together to form phrases or sentences

theater: a large area where a war is fought

LEARN MORE

Kallen, Stuart A. *Navajo Code Talkers.* Minneapolis: Lerner Publications, 2018.

National Geographic Kids: 10 Facts about World War 2
https://www.natgeokids.com/za/discover/history/general
-history/world-war-two/

National Museum of the American Indian: Native Words, Native Warriors
https://americanindian.si.edu/education/codetalkers/html
/index.html

Navajo Nation Government: History
https://www.navajo-nsn.gov/history.htm

Owens, Lisa L. *World War II Code Breakers.* Minneapolis: Lerner Publications, 2019.

Shoup, Kate. *Life as a Navajo Code Talker in World War II.* New York: Cavendish Square, 2018.

INDEX